THE GATHERING OF THE LIGHTS

Ian Dannatt

Copyright © 2023 Ian Dannatt
All rights reserved.
ISBN:
ISBN 9798372885271

CONTENTS

The Start Of Memories Recalled 5
From Books Of Devotion 6
No Chains To Hold 7
What Is My Truth 8
With Your Eyes To The Back Wall 9
With Words Deeply Buried 10
I Feel Like Dying 11
Open The Clock Case 12
The Past Called Me 13
There Is Truth In Our Hearts 14
Expecting To Fall 15
The Shell Of A Man 16
Will Lights And Snow Bring Sparkling Joy 17
Eyes That Sparkle And Reflect 18
Misty Images Beckoning 19
Tears Will Be The Costume 20
When Snow Separates Us 21
The Company 22
My Face A Map 23
This Stupid Old World 24
Three Wishes For You 25
The Gangsters Of Hilltop 26
Happiness Not Sad 27
To Heal The Last 28
My Unlucky Kingdom Of Pain 29
Christmas Lights 30
The Very Centre Of My Loving Heart 31
The Gathering Of The Lights 32
Light Is The Hope 33
The Mountains I Seeked So Long 34
Line Of Fire Line Of Snow 35
There's A World I Know 36
Al Capone Was Our Ancestor 37
The Hope In Our Hearts 38

THE START OF MEMORIES RECALLED

Opening a book
Is the start
Of memories
Recalled
All my books
Are scattered
Strangers
No brother
Of each other
Are they

Ghosts of spiders
Walk over me
(Spiders being
The deeds
We once did)
The fears
Gather like
Flies on meat
No help left
For me

FROM BOOKS OF DEVOTION

Call to me
From books
Of devotion
The Angel
That looks
Towards the
Last view
Of the narrow
Sea shore
Called hope

I walk along
With death
But not too
Close a step
The grains
Of sand hurt
My heart
Each one a soul
That once loved
Now lost

NO CHAINS TO HOLD

How it hangs
In the air
Like my hope
No chains
To hold
How can both
Stay there
Without them
Crashing down

Where will I go
After rain
Kills my mood
Rather than
Uplift it
Casting aside
Memories of you
I falsely write
A new life
I once lived

WHAT IS MY TRUTH

What is my truth
Can I tell how
It differs from
My fucking lie

How it frees my
Imagination
To think there is
A difference

WITH YOUR EYES TO THE BACK WALL

Hold me with
Your eyes to
The back wall
So no other
Face will you
Look on fondly
As you love me

Why does my
Throat burn
When it's my
Eyes that cry
Acid tears
Fears turn our
Love rotten

WITH WORDS DEEPLY BURIED

Sometimes I skate along
On smooth ice
With words easily seen
Other times I trudge
Through thick snow
With words deeply buried

Like the Lady of Shallot
Realising the curse
Had arrived as foretold.
The spectre of inspiration
Has risen from its body
Here to haunt and mock me

I FEEL LIKE DYING

I feel like dying
But crying will
Bring me back
To equilibrium

The ray of hope
Is fading now
Can you light
A new candle?

OPEN THE CLOCK CASE

Open the clock case
And feel the time
With curious fingers
Making the passage
From clear to unknown
More real and personal

Reading brings tears
Summons the past
That kills the heart
All senses lead me
To sad disaster born
All tears flow from me

THE PAST CALLED ME

The sadness
Of living
When alive
I am not

Oh the past
Called me
Another name
Now lost

THERE IS TRUTH IN OUR HEARTS

There is truth
In our hearts
Permanently
The lies only
Lodgers living
Temporarily

The applause
Is not always
For you love
But what a
Beautiful soul
You are to me

EXPECTING TO FALL

I spend my life
In utter despair
Nails long so to
Hang onto the cliff
Expecting to fall
One day I will

If I fear to stay
Icy pitiful times
Will be our fate
The tambourine
Sounds a beat
Until death calls

THE SHELL OF A MAN

I'm a sad little boy
Lonely and afraid
Hidden within
The shell of a man

No monsters live
Beneath my bed
So tell me now
Why I am so afraid

WILL LIGHTS AND SNOW BRING SPARKLING JOY

Will there be
A Christmas time
This year for me
Will lights and snow
Bring sparkling joy
As music sacred
Or profane sings
Out to the world
As my eyes close

Coloured paper
Tell a story that's old
Of anticipation
A little boy's wish
To dream again
That there is
Father Christmas
Out there real
Not just a dream

EYES THAT SPARKLE AND REFLECT

Let's get rid
Of these days
The hours are
Too long for me
They stand in
Front of my happy
State of mind

Over the hill
I see flowers
That comfort
Light in colour
That match the
Eyes that sparkle
And reflect

MISTY IMAGES BECKONING

Today is always
Tomorrow
Never for me
Yesterday

No memories
To look back on
Just misty images
Beckoning

TEARS WILL BE THE COSTUME

I cry enough
To not bother
With laughter
Tears will be
The costume
To match my part
Both happy or sad

Face so bright
The dark heart
Hides away
Though I wish
The day was
Finally over for me
Time to sleep tight

WHEN SNOW SEPARATES US

When snow
Separates us
Icy tears
Flow down
Slowly turning
Us to crystal
Statues sighing

Green fields of
Forgetfulness
Awaken me
With their call
Time to go home
With friends
Supportive close

THE COMPANY

I was born in a
Company house
On the edge of a
Company town
My future was to be
A company man

Now lonely is
The company
I work for now
My world ended
Turned to a Stranger's
Playground

MY FACE A MAP

My face a map
Formed by
Expert forgers
Showing the way
To certain joy
But leading only
To dark tears

The sadness is
Too painful
Though in a
Deep dark well
So you're led
To sunny fields
Of joyfulness

THIS STUPID OLD WORLD

I danced
Quite dazed
For a while
To music
Of strife

What is it
I should know
To love again
This stupid
Old world

THREE WISHES FOR YOU

Three wishes
For you
None for me
I have you
That was my
Wish come true

The world is
Cruel to
The innocent
In times of
Fairy tales told
Let reality win

THE GANGSTERS OF HILLTOP

Back together
The team
Thought lost
The long walk
Beckons
To cake or biscuits

HAPPINESS NOT SAD

A new year begins
With the arrival of a
First few small tears
May they remain ones
Of happiness not sad

Odd is the year
Though very even
Is our temperament
And though it's winter
We somehow feel warm

TO HEAL THE LOST

Go the times
To worlds
Of trouble
Troubling me
To heal the lost

The company
I did not
Seek today
I will need to
Have tomorrow

MY UNLUCKY KINGDOM OF PAIN

All subjects
LIve sad
Stupid lives
Shut off afraid
Hidden from view
No company
Here soothes me
To break the
Hellish icy fear

Come to me
From the
Land of luck
That you rule
To my unlucky
Kingdom of pain
Extend your empire
By destroying
My sorry land

CHRISTMAS LIGHTS

Only a few more days
Of Christmas lights
Before each one
Winks out dying
What then will help
Banish my darkness?

I will close my eyes
So I will not see
Through my own
Will and Intention
Rather than the dark
Imposing blindness

THE VERY CENTRE OF MY LOVING HEART

The aching sadness
That resides legally
In the very centre
Of my loving heart
Never to be evicted
No matter the fear
And utter panic
That causes pain

Over the waterfall
Time has flowed
The chance ends
For any peaceful
Existence for me
Soon the deep
Soothing waters
Will take me back

THE GATHERING OF THE LIGHTS

The gathering of the lights
To mark the end of Christmas
The start of dull darkness
Before the arrival of spring

Where shall we go my love
To be always covered in green
With daisy chains linked
To connect our two hearts

LIGHT IS THE HOPE

If I hated
Myself
A lot less
Could you
Love me
A little bit
More please

Heavy is
Heart
Light is
The hope
That love
Will finally
Be my friend

THE MOUNTAINS I SEEKED SO LONG

I stand in front
Of the mountains
I seeked so long
To achieve peace
Now it's too late
The summit is
Forever forbidden

Thoughts are not
Your friend this day
They nig and nag
Until all peace dies
Your sanity lost
In the valley
The gods laugh

LINE OF FIRE LINE OF SNOW

Line of fire
Line of snow
Burn me
Freeze me
Cast me in hell
Leave me
Emotionally dead

I strive to
See my soul
Amongst
The greenest
Fields all calm
Still I hover
Cold and blistered

THERE'S A WORLD I KNOW

There's a
World I know
A world of
Lasting beauty
One we gaze on
With wonder
And creeping dread

One day a
Song I'll sing
Of flowers
Blooming soft
Sending scents
Of hopefulness
That soothes and heals

AL CAPONE WAS OUR ANCESTOR

The Hilltop
Is our Sunday
Gangsters hideout
Safe from the
Forces of law

But the Feds
Are close by
Rushing to arrest
Leading us to
Scatter and flee

THE HOPE IN OUR HEARTS

Sometimes
The hope
In our hearts
Goes missing
Leaving despair
To end our
Days with
Utterly lost

I aim to go
Find mine
In a place
They say
Is called
Never been
Never seen
Just a dream

Printed in Great Britain
by Amazon